# IN HER HOUR OF NEED

## MESSAGES OF STRENGTH & HOPE

## Also By Anthony D Brice

*Poor Me to Soul Rich: Upgrade Your Mindset to Maximize Your Health, Multiply Your Wealth & Magnify Your Relationships*

*Loving Alone Until We're Together: Discover the 4 Magnets for Maximum Attraction to Manifest True Love*

*My Reflection: A Journal for Healing, Self-Discovery, and Living on Purpose*

*I Am Powerful, I Am Amazing, I Am a King*

# IN HER HOUR OF NEED

## MESSAGES OF STRENGTH & HOPE

Anthony D Brice

The Impower Group, LLC.

# CONTENTS

Chapter 6

## Hope: Light at the End of the Tunnel 73

# INTRODUCTION

If you're holding this book, it's likely because you're navigating a season of heartbreak. Perhaps you're feeling the sting of a recent breakup, or maybe you're grappling with the aftermath of a relationship that didn't pan out as you'd hoped. You might even feel like you're the only one who's ever felt this way, that no one else could possibly understand the depth of your pain.

But I want you to know something crucial: *You are not alone.*

I see you. I see the woman who's spent countless nights staring at the ceiling, a well of silent tears blurring her vision. I see the woman who locks herself in the car, just to scream out her frustrations where no one can hear. I see the woman who feels like she's losing herself in the endless routine, yearning for a taste of the vibrant spirit she once was. I see you, and I understand.

This book, "In Her Hour of Need: Messages of Strength and Hope," is for you. It's a collection of messages that I hope will bring you comfort, strength, and hope in your hour of need. It's a reminder that even in the darkest times, there's always a light at the end of the tunnel. And most importantly, it's a testament to the incredible strength and resilience of women like you.

You might be wondering, "Why should I listen to him? He's a man." And you're right. I am a man. But I was raised by a young single mother, grew up in the house with my grandmother, and had many loving aunts. They all played important roles in raising me and have shaped the empathy I have for the female experience. I've seen the pain, the heartbreak, and the resilience. I've been the shoulder to cry on, the confidant, the friend. And over the past decade, thousands of women have confided in me, asked for advice, and praised me for helping them through hard times with my positive messages on social media.

In the pages that follow, we'll have a heart-to-heart about heartbreak, healing, self-love, vulnerability, empowerment, and hope. We'll talk about the tough stuff, but we'll also celebrate the victories, no matter how small. And through it all, I hope you'll come to see that you are more than enough, just as you are.

So, if you're feeling lost, if you're in pain, or if you're just in need of a little hope, this book is for you. Because in your hour of need, you deserve messages of strength and hope. Let's begin this journey together.

# CHAPTER ONE

# HEART-TO-HEART ON HEARTBREAK

Heartbreak is a universal experience, yet it's one of the most personal things we can go through. It's like a storm that sweeps through your life, leaving you feeling lost and disoriented in its wake. You might be feeling a deep sense of loss, a hollow emptiness where love once resided. You might be grappling with feelings of betrayal, disappointment, or a profound sadness that feels as if it might never lift.

But here's something I want you to hold onto: It's okay to feel this way. Your feelings are valid. Your pain is real. And most importantly, you're not alone in this.

In this chapter, we're going to have a heart-to-heart about heartbreak. We'll talk about the reality of heartbreak, the silent battles you might be fighting, and the beginning of the healing process. We'll discuss the importance of acknowledging your feelings and the power that lies in doing so.

And through it all, I'll be sharing messages of hope and strength. Because even in the midst of heartbreak, there's always hope. There's always a way forward. And there's always a strength within you, waiting to be discovered.

So, let's begin this conversation. Let's talk about heartbreak, not as something to be feared or avoided, but as a part of our human experience. And let's do it together, with compassion, understanding, and a shared hope for healing.

## Section 1: The Reality of Heartbreak

Heartbreak is a storm. It's a whirlwind of emotions that can leave you feeling as if you're adrift in a sea of pain and confusion. It's the sharp sting of loss, the hollow emptiness where love once resided, the echoes of shared laughter and intimate whispers that now seem to mock you with their absence.

It's the questions that keep you up at night, the what-ifs and the whys that replay over and over in your mind. It's the self-doubt that creeps in, making you question your worth, your choices, your very identity.

It's the physical ache in your chest, the tears that seem to come from nowhere, the moments when you forget they're gone and reach for the phone to share a thought, a joke, a piece of your day.

And it's the loneliness. The feeling of being alone in a crowd, of being disconnected from the world around you. The sense that no one else could possibly understand the depth of your pain.

But here's the thing: Heartbreak, as painful as it is, is also a testament to our capacity to love and to feel. It's a testament to our humanity. And while it might not feel like it right now, it's also the first step on the path to healing.

So, if you're in the throes of heartbreak, know this: It's okay to feel this way. It's okay to grieve, to cry, to rage against the unfairness of it all. Your feelings are valid. Your pain is real. And you're not alone.

In the following sections, we'll explore the silent battles that often accompany heartbreak, and we'll begin to discuss the healing process. But for now, allow yourself to acknowledge the reality of your heartbreak. Because in doing so, you're taking the first step towards healing

## Section 2: The Silent Battles

In the aftermath of heartbreak, there are battles that are fought in silence. These are the struggles that others may not see, the internal conflicts that can feel just as real and painful as any physical wound.

There's the battle against loneliness, the feeling of isolation that can be so overwhelming it feels like a physical weight. There's the battle against self-doubt, the nagging voice in your head that whispers you're not enough, that you're to blame, that you could have done more.

There's the battle against memories, the fight to keep the past from flooding your present. The struggle to not let the happy moments make you question your decision, or the painful ones make you doubt your worth.

There's the battle against hope, the dangerous glimmer that maybe things could be different, that maybe they'll change, that maybe you can go back to the way things were.

And then there's the battle against yourself, the struggle to not lose who you are amidst the storm of heartbreak.

These battles are tough. They're exhausting. And they're often fought in silence, behind a smile, beneath a "I'm fine."

But here's the thing: It's okay to fight these battles. It's okay to struggle, to stumble, to fall. Because in every battle, there's a chance for growth, for learning, for strength.

And remember, you're not fighting these battles alone. In the following sections, we'll discuss how to navigate the healing process and how to turn these silent battles into stepping stones towards a stronger, more resilient you.

But for now, know this: Your battles are valid. Your struggles are real. And you're stronger than you think.

## Section 3: The Healing Process Begins

Healing is a journey, not a destination. It's a process that unfolds over time, often in ways that are unexpected and unpredictable. It's not a straight line, but a winding path with ups and downs, progress and setbacks.

The healing process begins when you acknowledge your pain. When you allow yourself to feel your feelings, to grieve your loss, to mourn what could have been. It begins when you give yourself permission to hurt, to cry, to rage, to feel.

It continues when you start to take care of yourself. When you nourish your body, rest your mind, and nurture your spirit. When you do things that bring you joy, that make you feel alive, that remind you of who you are.

It deepens when you start to let go. When you release the past, forgive yourself, forgive them. When you accept that things have changed, that you have changed, and that change can be a beginning, not just an end.

And it culminates when you start to love yourself again. When you recognize your worth, your strength, your resilience. When you realize that you are enough, just as you are, and that you deserve love, respect, and happiness.

The healing process is unique to each person. It takes time, patience, and a lot of self-love. In the following sections, we'll explore ways to navigate this process and to turn your pain into strength.

But for now, know this: It's okay to start healing. It's

okay to take your time. And it's okay to be gentle with yourself. Because healing is not about "getting over" your heartbreak, but about learning to live with it, and in doing so, finding a new way forward.

## Section 4: The Power of Acknowledgement

In the middle of heartbreak, it's easy to fall into the trap of denial or avoidance. We might try to push our feelings away, to bury them under a facade of "I'm fine" or "It doesn't matter." We might try to distract ourselves, to fill our days with busyness in the hope that we can outrun our pain. But the truth is, healing doesn't begin with avoidance; it begins with acknowledgement

Acknowledging your feelings is like shining a light into the darkness. It's about seeing your pain for what it is, not as something to be feared or avoided, but as a part of your human experience. It's about saying, "Yes, I'm hurting. Yes, this is hard. And it's okay to feel this way."

Acknowledgement is not about wallowing in your pain or letting it consume you. It's about giving yourself permission to feel, to grieve, to be human. It's about validating your own experiences, your own emotions. And it's about recognizing that it's okay to not be okay sometimes.

When you acknowledge your feelings, you take away their power to control you. You allow yourself to feel them, to experience them, and then, when you're ready, to let them go. You give yourself the freedom to heal at your own pace, in your own way.

So, if you're feeling lost in the storm of heartbreak, I encourage you to take a moment to acknowledge your feelings. Allow yourself to feel your pain, your sadness, your anger. Validate your own experiences. And remember, it's okay to not be okay. You're human.

In the next section, we'll explore uplifting messages of hope and strength. But for now, remember the power of acknowledgement. Because in acknowledging your feelings, you're taking a powerful step towards healing.

## Section 5: Messages of Hope

When you're going through heartbreak, it can sometimes feel like you're lost in a dark tunnel with no end in sight. But I want you to remember something important: Even in the darkest tunnel, there's always a light at the end. And that light is hope.

Hope is the belief that things can get better. It's the faith in your own strength and resilience. It's the knowledge that, no matter how hard things are right now, you have the power to overcome.

So, as you navigate your heartbreak, I want to share some messages of hope with you:

1. **You are stronger than you think.** You may feel broken now, but remember that broken crayons still color. You still have so much beauty, strength, and potential within you.

2. **This pain is temporary.** It may not feel like it now, but the pain you're feeling is not permanent. With time, patience, and self-care, you will heal.

3. **You are not alone.** Even if it feels like it, remember that you're not alone in your pain. There are others who have been where you are and have come out the other side stronger and wiser.

**4. You are worthy of love.** Your worth is not determined by someone else's inability to see it. You are deserving of a love that is kind, respectful, and reciprocated.

**5. There is growth in pain.** Heartbreak, as painful as it is, can also be a powerful catalyst for growth. It can teach us about ourselves, about what we want and don't want, and about the strength we have within us.

**6. You have the power to create the life you want.** Heartbreak can feel like an ending, but it can also be a beginning. It's an opportunity to reassess, to rebuild, and to create a life that aligns with your values and desires.

Remember these messages of hope as you navigate your heartbreak. Hold onto them in your darkest moments. And know that, no matter how hard things are right now, you have the strength and the resilience to overcome.

## Final Thoughts on Heartbreak

We've journeyed through the reality of heartbreak, acknowledging its pain and the silent battles it often brings. We've begun to understand that it's okay to feel, to grieve, and to acknowledge our pain. And through it all, I hope you've found some comfort in the messages of hope and strength shared.

Remember, heartbreak is not your final destination. It's a part of your journey, a testament to your capacity to love and feel deeply. And while it's painful, it's also the first step towards healing. As we move forward, know that you're not alone. You are stronger than you think, and there's a light at the end of this tunnel.

# CHAPTER TWO

## LET'S TALK ABOUT HEALING

If you've made it to this chapter, it means you've taken the first step towards healing. You've acknowledged your heartbreak, you've allowed yourself to feel the pain, and now, you're ready to start the journey towards healing. And for that, I want to say: I'm proud of you.

Healing is a journey, not a destination. It's a process that takes time, patience, and a lot of self-love. It's not linear, and it's not always easy. There will be days when you feel like you're making progress, and there will be days when you feel like you're back at square one. And that's okay. It's all part of the process.

In this chapter, we're going to talk about healing. We'll discuss what it really means to heal, the different stages of healing, and the importance of self-care during the healing process. We'll also explore the role of forgiveness in healing, and how it can help you move forward.

And as always, I'll be sharing messages of hope and

strength. Because no matter where you are in your healing journey, there's always hope. There's always a way forward. And there's always a strength within you, waiting to be discovered.

So, let's begin this conversation. Let's talk about healing, not as something to be feared or avoided, but as a part of our human experience. And let's do it together, with compassion, understanding, and a shared hope for healing.

## Section 1: Understanding Healing

Healing. It's a word we hear a lot, especially when we're dealing with heartbreak. But what does it really mean to heal? And how do we start the healing process?

First, let's debunk a common myth: Healing is not about "getting over" your heartbreak. It's not about forgetting the person who hurt you, or pretending that the relationship never happened. It's not a process with a clear beginning and end, and it's certainly not a race.

Healing is a journey. It's about acknowledging your pain, understanding your emotions, and learning to navigate life with your heartbreak as part of your story. It's about finding ways to cope, to grow, and to find joy and meaning in life again.

Healing is also deeply personal. What works for one person might not work for another. There's no "right" way to heal, and there's no set timeline for how long it should take. It's okay to take your time, to have good days and bad days, to feel like you're making progress one moment and like you're back at square one the next.

Most importantly, healing is not something you have to do alone. It's okay to ask for help, to lean on the people who care about you, to seek professional support if you need it. You don't have to carry your pain by yourself.

In the following sections, we'll explore the different stages of healing, the importance of self-care during the healing process, and the role of forgiveness in healing. But for now, remember this: Healing is a journey, and it's okay to take it one step at a time.

## Section 2: The Stages of Healing

Healing isn't a straight path from point A to point B. It's a journey that often involves taking two steps forward and one step back. It's a process that's unique to each individual, with its own timeline and progression.

That being said, there are certain stages of healing that many people experience. Understanding these stages can help you make sense of what you're going through and give you a roadmap for your healing journey.

1. **Shock and Denial:** This is the initial stage where the reality of the heartbreak hasn't fully sunk in. You might find yourself in disbelief, unable to accept what's happened.

2. **Pain and Guilt:** As the shock wears off, it's replaced by a period of intense pain and guilt. You might replay the relationship over and over in your mind, questioning your actions and blaming yourself for what happened.

3. **Anger and Bargaining:** In this stage, you might feel a surge of anger towards your ex-partner or the situation. You might also find yourself bargaining, imagining "what if" scenarios that could have saved the relationship.

4. **Depression and Loneliness:** This is a period of

reflection and sadness. You might feel a deep sense of loss and loneliness, as you fully comprehend the magnitude of what's happened.

5. **The Upward Turn:** Gradually, the intense pain begins to lessen. You start adjusting to life without your ex-partner and the depression starts to lift.

6. **Reconstruction and Working Through:** In this stage, you start to become more functional in your everyday life and begin to work through the residual feelings of loss and sadness.

7. **Acceptance and Hope:** This is the final stage where you accept what's happened and start to look forward to the future. You realize that there is life after heartbreak and begin to feel hopeful about what's to come.

Remember, these stages are not set in stone. You might not go through all of them, or you might go through them in a different order. You might even find yourself cycling back and forth between stages. And that's okay. Healing is a personal journey, and it's different for everyone.

In the next section, we'll talk about the importance of self-care during the healing process. But for now, remember this: No matter what stage you're in, you're making progress. And with each step you take, you're moving closer towards healing.

## Section 3: Self-Care During Healing

When you're navigating the choppy waters of heartbreak, it's easy to forget about taking care of yourself. But self-care is not just about bubble baths and spa days (although those can be great!). It's about nurturing your mind, body, and spirit in ways that support your healing journey.

First and foremost, self-care is about giving yourself permission to feel. It's about acknowledging your emotions without judgment, allowing yourself to grieve, and giving yourself the space to process your feelings. It's okay to cry. It's okay to be angry. It's okay to not be okay. These are all normal, valid responses to heartbreak

Self-care is also about taking care of your physical health. This might mean ensuring you're eating healthy foods, getting regular exercise, and getting enough sleep. It might also mean seeking medical help if your heartbreak is affecting your physical health.

But self-care doesn't stop there. It's also about nurturing your spirit. This might mean spending time in nature, practicing mindfulness or meditation, or engaging in activities that bring you joy and peace. It might mean seeking support from trusted friends or a professional counselor. It might mean setting boundaries to protect your energy and your peace.

And perhaps most importantly, self-care is about being kind to yourself. It's about treating yourself with the same compassion and understanding you'd offer a friend going through a similar situation. It's about reminding yourself that you're doing the best you can, and that's enough.

During heartbreak, self-care can feel like a lifeline. It's a way to nurture and support yourself as you navigate your healing journey. So, as you move forward, I encourage you to make self-care a priority. Because you're worth it.

## Section 4: The Role of Forgiveness in Healing

Forgiveness. It's a word that can stir up a lot of emotions. For some, it might feel like a relief, a release of a heavy burden. For others, it might feel like an impossible task, a mountain too steep to climb. But here's the thing about forgiveness: it's not about the other person. It's about you. It's about freeing yourself from the chains of resentment and bitterness that can hold you back from healing.

Now, let's be clear. Forgiveness doesn't mean forgetting what happened or excusing the actions of the person who hurt you. It doesn't mean you have to let that person back into your life or pretend that everything is okay. What it does mean is letting go of the anger and resentment that's keeping you stuck in the past, so you can move forward.

Forgiving someone who hurt you is one of the hardest things you'll ever do. But it's also one of the most powerful. Because when you forgive, you take back your power. You reclaim your right to heal, to grow, to move on.

And let's not forget about self-forgiveness. Often, we are our own harshest critics. We blame ourselves for what happened, for not seeing the signs, for not doing enough. But holding onto self-blame and guilt only serves to keep us stuck in our pain. By forgiving ourselves, we acknowledge that we did the best we could with the knowledge and resources we had at the time. And we give ourselves permission to learn, to grow, and to heal.

In the end, forgiveness is a gift you give to yourself. It's a key part of the healing process, a step towards freeing yourself from the pain of the past. And while it might not be easy, it's a journey worth taking. Because you deserve to heal. You deserve to move forward. And you deserve to find peace.

## Section 5: Messages of Hope

As we navigate the path of healing, it's important to keep hope alive. Hope is the light that guides us through our darkest times. It's the belief that better days are ahead, even when we can't quite see them yet. It's the strength that keeps us moving forward, even when we're weary.

So, as you embark on your healing journey, here are some messages of hope to carry with you:

**You are stronger than you think.** You've already shown incredible strength by acknowledging your heartbreak and beginning this journey of healing. Remember that strength in the moments when you feel weak.

**Healing is not linear.** There will be ups and downs, good days and bad. That's okay. It's all part of the process. Don't beat yourself up if you have a setback. Just keep moving forward.

**You are not alone.** Even when it feels like you're the only one going through this, remember that you're not. There are others who have walked this path before you, and there are people who care about you and want to support you.

**You are worthy of love and happiness.** Heartbreak can

make us question our worth, but remember this: You are worthy of love. You are worthy of happiness. And you are worthy of a relationship that brings you joy, not pain.

**Better days are ahead.** It might not feel like it now, but better days are coming. You will heal. You will grow. And you will come out of this stronger and wiser than before.

Hold onto these messages of hope as you continue your healing journey. Remember them in the moments when you feel lost or alone. And most importantly, remember that you have the strength to heal, to grow, and to find happiness again.

## Final Thoughts on Healing

In this chapter, we've begun to explore the healing process. We've talked about what healing really means, the stages of healing, the importance of self-care, and the role of forgiveness. And through it all, I hope you've found some comfort and hope in the messages shared.

Healing is a journey, and it's one that takes time, patience, and a lot of self-love. But remember, you have the strength to heal, to grow, and to emerge from this experience stronger and more resilient than before. As we continue this journey together, hold onto the hope and strength within you. You are more than your heartbreak. You are healing, and that's something to celebrate.

# CHAPTER THREE

# THE SELF-LOVE CHAT

There's a phrase that's often thrown around in self-help books and motivational speeches: "You have to love yourself first." But what does that really mean? And why is it so important?

Self-love is more than just a buzzword. It's a fundamental aspect of our wellbeing, a cornerstone of our mental and emotional health. It's about recognizing your worth, honoring your needs, and treating yourself with the same kindness and respect you'd offer to someone you care about.

But let's be honest: self-love isn't always easy. It's a journey, and like any journey, it has its highs and lows. There might be times when you stumble, when you struggle to see your worth, when you find it hard to love the person you see in the mirror. And that's okay. It's all part of the process.

In this chapter, we're going to have a chat about self-love. We'll explore what it means, why it's important, and how you can cultivate it in your own life. We'll talk about the role of self-love in healing, and I'll share some practical tips and exercises to help you on your journey.

And through it all, I'll be sharing messages of self-love and self-acceptance. Because no matter where you are on your journey, you deserve to be loved - especially by yourself.

So, let's begin this conversation. Let's talk about self-love, not as something to be achieved or earned, but as a gift to be given - to yourself, from yourself.

## Section 1: Understanding Self-Love

When we talk about self-love, what do we really mean? Is it about treating ourselves to a spa day or indulging in our favorite foods? Is it about repeating positive affirmations in the mirror? While these things can be part of self-love, they only scratch the surface of what it truly means.

Self-love is about recognizing your worth and treating yourself with the same kindness and respect you would offer to someone you care about. It's about acknowledging your needs and taking steps to meet them. It's about setting boundaries and not allowing others to treat you poorly. It's about celebrating your achievements, however small, and not being too hard on yourself when things don't go as planned.

Self-love is not about being selfish or narcissistic. It's not about ignoring your flaws or pretending they don't exist. Instead, it's about accepting yourself as you are, flaws and all, and understanding that you are a work in progress.

Self-love is also not a destination, but a journey. It's a process that requires patience, effort, and a lot of compassion towards oneself. And it's a journey that is unique to each individual. What works for one person might not work for another, and that's okay. The important thing is to find what works for you.

Understanding self-love is the first step towards cultivating it. In the following sections, we'll explore this journey and how self-love can aid in the healing process.

But for now, take a moment to reflect on your own understanding of self-love. What does it mean to you? And how can you incorporate more of it into your life

## Section 2: The Journey to Self-Love

The journey to self-love is a deeply personal one. It's a path that is unique to each of us, shaped by our experiences, our beliefs, and our relationships. It's a journey that can be challenging, sometimes even painful, but it's also one of the most rewarding journeys you can embark on.

For many of us, the journey to self-love begins with a decision. A decision to prioritize our own well-being, to honor our needs and desires, to treat ourselves with the same kindness and compassion that we extend to others. It's a decision to acknowledge our worth, to recognize that we are deserving of love and respect, not because of what we do or how we look, but simply because we exist.

But making the decision is just the first step. The journey to self-love is a winding road filled with wins and setbacks. There will be days when you feel confident and empowered, and there will be days when you struggle with self-doubt and criticism. And that's okay.

What's important is that you keep progressing. That you continue to show up for yourself, even on the hard days. That you remind yourself, over and over again, that you are worthy of love and respect. That you are enough, just as you are.

We're all walking this path together, each of us learning and growing in our own way. So, as you embark on your journey to self-love, know that you're in good company. And know that you have the strength and the courage to navigate this path, one step at a time.

## Section 3: The Role of Self-Love in Healing

When we're on our healing journey, it's easy to lose sight of our own worth. We might find ourselves questioning our value, our attractiveness, even our lovability. But here's the truth: You are worthy. You are valuable. You are lovable. And one of the most powerful ways to reinforce these truths is through self-love.

Self-love is like an ointment for the wounds of heartbreak. It soothes the pain, eases the sting, and helps us to heal from the inside out. When we love ourselves, we're better able to process our emotions, to learn from our experiences, and to move forward with strength and grace.

But how does self-love do this? Let's break it down:

**Self-love validates our emotions:** When we love ourselves, we acknowledge our feelings as valid and important. We allow ourselves to grieve, to be angry, to be sad. This validation is a crucial part of the healing process.

**Self-love fosters self-compassion:** Self-love encourages us to be gentle with ourselves, to treat ourselves with the same kindness and understanding we'd offer to a friend. This self-compassion can help us to heal more effectively.

**Self-love promotes growth:** When we love ourselves, we're more likely to see our experiences - even painful ones - as opportunities for growth. We're more likely to learn from our heartbreak and to use it as steps towards a stronger, healthier future.

**Self-love strengthens our resilience:** Self-love helps us to build resilience, equipping us to face future challenges with courage and confidence. It reminds us of our strength, our worth, and our ability to overcome.

In the next section, we'll explore some practical ways to cultivate self-love. But for now, I want you to remember this: Self-love is not a luxury. It's not a bonus or an extra. It's a necessity. It's a vital part of the healing process. And it's something that every single one of us deserves.

## Section 4: Practical Ways to Cultivate Self-Love

Self-love isn't something that happens overnight. It's a process that requires time, patience, and a lot of compassion for yourself. But the good news is, there are practical steps you can take to cultivate self-love in your daily life. Here are some suggestions:

1. **Practice Self-Care:** This can be anything that makes you feel good and nurtures your physical, emotional, or mental well-being. It could be taking a relaxing bath, going for a walk in nature, meditating, or even just taking a few moments for yourself.

2. **Set Boundaries:** Learning to say no is a powerful act of self-love. It's about respecting your own time, energy, and emotional capacity. Remember, it's okay to prioritize your own needs.

3. **Use Affirmations:** Positive affirmations can help to rewire your brain and change negative thought patterns. Try to start each day by saying something positive to yourself, like "I am worthy of love and kindness," or "I am enough, just as I am."

4. **Practice Mindfulness:** Being present and fully engaged in the current moment can help you to cultivate a deeper appreciation for yourself and your life. Try to incorporate

mindfulness practices into your daily routine, such as mindful eating, mindful walking, or simply taking a few moments to focus on your breath.

5. **Celebrate Your Achievements:** No matter how small they may seem, it's important to acknowledge and celebrate your achievements. This can help to boost your self-esteem and reinforce your sense of self-worth.

6. **Seek Support When Needed:** Remember, it's okay to ask for help. Whether it's from a trusted friend, a family member, or a professional, seeking support is a sign of strength, not weakness.

Remember, self-love is about making small, consistent changes that add up over time. So be patient with yourself and remember to celebrate your progress along the way.

## Section 5: Messages of Self-Love

In this section, we're going to focus on the most important relationship you'll ever have - the one with yourself. It's easy to lose sight of this relationship, especially when you're dealing with heartbreak. But it's during these times that self-love becomes even more crucial.

Let's start with a simple truth: **You are enough**. You are worthy of love, respect, and happiness, just as you are. You don't need to change for anyone. You don't need to shrink yourself to fit into someone else's idea of who you should be. You are enough, just as you are.

Self-love isn't about being selfish or narcissistic. It's about recognizing your worth and treating yourself with the same kindness and respect you'd give to someone you care about. It's about setting boundaries and not allowing others to treat you poorly. It's about taking care of your physical, emotional, and mental well-being.

Here are some messages of self-love that I want you to remember:

**You are not defined by your past or your mistakes.** Everyone makes mistakes. Everyone has things in their past they wish they could change. But these things don't define you. You are not your past. You are not your mistakes. You are a person who is constantly growing and learning.

**It's okay to put yourself first.** This is something many women struggle with. We're often taught to put others' needs before our own. But it's not selfish to take care of yourself. In fact, it's necessary. You can't pour from an empty cup. You need to take care of yourself first, so you can be there for others.

**You deserve to be treated with respect.** Don't settle for less than you deserve. Don't let anyone treat you poorly or make you feel less than. You deserve to be treated with kindness and respect.

**You are stronger than you think.** You've been through heartbreak. You've been through pain. And you're still here. You're still standing. That takes incredible strength. Don't ever underestimate yourself.

**You are beautiful, inside and out.** Don't let anyone make you feel otherwise. You are beautiful, just as you are. Your beauty isn't just physical - it's in your kindness, your compassion, your resilience.

Remember these messages. Write them down. Repeat them to yourself. Because you deserve to love yourself, just as you are.

## Final Thoughts on Self-Love

As we wrap up this chapter, I want you to take a moment to reflect on everything we've discussed. Self-love isn't just about bubble baths and treating yourself to your favorite dessert (although those things can certainly be part of it!). It's about acknowledging your worth, honoring your needs, and treating yourself with the same kindness and respect you'd show to a loved one.

Remember, the journey to self-love isn't always linear. There will be days when you feel on top of the world, and others when you struggle to find a single positive thing to say about yourself. That's okay. It's all part of the process. The important thing is that you keep going, keep trying, keep believing in your worth.

And on those tough days, I hope you'll come back to this chapter. I hope you'll read these words and remember that you are deserving of love and kindness, especially from yourself. I hope you'll remember that self-love is not a destination, but a journey, and every step you take on this path, no matter how small, is a victory.

So, keep going. Keep loving yourself, in all your imperfect, human glory. Because you are worth it. And this journey to self-love? It's one of the most important journeys you'll ever take.

# CHAPTER FOUR

# STRENGTH IN BEING VULNERABLE

Vulnerability. It's a word that can stir up a lot of emotions. For many of us, it's associated with fear, discomfort, and risk. We live in a world that often equates vulnerability with weakness, that encourages us to build walls around our hearts and hide our true selves.

But what if I told you that vulnerability is not a weakness, but a strength? That opening up, letting down your guard, and showing your true self can be one of the most powerful things you can do?

In this chapter, we're going to explore the strength in being vulnerable. We'll talk about what it means to be vulnerable, the courage it takes to let yourself be seen, and the power that can come from embracing your vulnerability. We'll also discuss how vulnerability can lead to deeper connections with others and open up new possibilities for growth and healing.

And through it all, I'll be sharing messages of strength

and courage. Because even in the face of fear and uncertainty, there's always a strength within you, waiting to be discovered.

So, let's begin this conversation. Let's talk about vulnerability, not as something to be feared or avoided, but as a testament to our strength and resilience. And let's do it with compassion, understanding, and a shared hope for healing.

## Section 1: Understanding Vulnerability

Vulnerability. It's a word that often carries with it a sense of fear and discomfort. We live in a world that often equates vulnerability with weakness, that tells us to build walls around our hearts and hide our true feelings. But what if I told you that vulnerability isn't a weakness at all? What if I told you that it's actually one of your greatest strengths?

Being vulnerable means allowing yourself to be seen, truly seen, in all your authenticity. It means opening up about your feelings, your fears, your hopes, and your dreams. It means letting go of the masks we often wear to protect ourselves, and instead, showing up as our true selves.

Yes, vulnerability can be scary. It can feel like standing on a stage, bare and exposed, with all eyes on you. It can feel like a risk, a leap of faith into the unknown. But it's also an act of courage. It's a testament to your strength and your resilience.

And here's the thing: Vulnerability is not about being weak or submissive. It's not about letting people walk all over you or take advantage of your openness. It's about being brave enough to show your true self, to express your feelings and needs, and to stand up for who you are.

So, if you're feeling scared or uncomfortable about being vulnerable, know this: It's okay to feel this way. Your feelings are valid. But also know that there's a strength in vulnerability, a power that comes from being authentically you. And that's something we'll explore more in the following sections.

## Section 2: The Courage to Be Vulnerable

Vulnerability is often seen as a weakness, but in reality, it requires immense courage. It's about allowing yourself to be seen, truly seen, in all your authenticity. It's about letting down your guard, peeling back the layers of protection you've built around your heart, and saying, "This is me. This is who I am."

It's not easy. It can feel scary and uncomfortable. You might fear judgment, rejection, or ridicule. You might worry that if people see the real you, they won't like what they see. But here's the thing: The courage to be vulnerable is not about being fearless. It's about feeling the fear and choosing to be open and authentic anyway.

Think about a time when you've opened up to someone, when you've shared something personal or revealed a part of yourself that you usually keep hidden. It might have been a moment of confession, a declaration of love, or a sharing of dreams and aspirations. How did it feel? Scary, perhaps. But also liberating, right?

That's the power of vulnerability. It's a courageous act of self-expression. It's a way of saying, "This is me, in all my complexity and uniqueness. This is my truth."

And here's another truth: You are worthy of being seen, heard, and loved for who you are. Your thoughts, feelings, and experiences matter. Your vulnerability is not a weakness; it's a strength. It's a testament to your courage, your authenticity, and your humanity.

So, as you navigate your journey of healing and self-discovery, I encourage you to embrace your vulnerability. Allow yourself to be seen. Allow yourself to be heard. Allow yourself to be authentically, courageously you.

## Section 3: The Power in Vulnerability

There's a common misconception that to be vulnerable is to expose your soft underbelly to the world, to invite hurt and rejection. But the truth is, vulnerability is one of the most powerful things you can embrace.

Vulnerability is about showing up and being seen. It's about letting go of the need to be perfect, to have it all together, to be anything other than who you truly are. It's about allowing yourself to be seen in your entirety, with all your strengths and all your flaws. And there's incredible power in that.

When you allow yourself to be vulnerable, you're saying, "This is me. This is who I am." You're asserting your worth, your value, your right to take up space in the world. And in doing so, you're challenging the narrative that you need to be anything other than yourself to be worthy of love and respect.

But the power in vulnerability doesn't stop there. When you're vulnerable, you give others permission to do the same. You create a space where authenticity is valued, where real connection can happen. You invite others to meet you in a place of honesty and openness, and in doing so, you open up the possibility for deeper, more meaningful connections.

So, if you're feeling scared to be vulnerable, know this: Your vulnerability is a testament to your strength. It's a testament to your courage, your authenticity, your humanity. And it's a testament to the incredible power that lies within you.

In the next section, we'll explore how vulnerability can lead to deeper connections with others. But for now, take a moment to acknowledge the power in your vulnerability. Because in doing so, you're taking a step towards embracing your true strength.

## Section 4: Vulnerability and Connection

When we allow ourselves to be vulnerable, we open up a space for genuine connection. It's in our most vulnerable moments that we reveal our true selves, our hopes, our fears, our dreams, and our insecurities. And it's in these moments that we can truly connect with others on a deep, meaningful level.

Think about it. The friendships that mean the most to you, the relationships that have shaped you – didn't they all involve a degree of vulnerability? Didn't they involve moments where you let your guard down, where you allowed yourself to be seen, blemishes and all?

Vulnerability is the bridge that connects two souls. It's the key that unlocks a deeper understanding, a deeper empathy. When you share your vulnerabilities with someone, you're not just sharing your weaknesses. You're sharing your humanity. And in doing so, you're inviting them to share theirs.

But here's the thing: Vulnerability is a two-way street. It involves not just sharing your own vulnerabilities, but also being receptive to those of others. It involves listening with an open heart and an open mind, offering empathy and understanding without judgment.

So, as you navigate your journey of healing, I encourage you to embrace vulnerability as a pathway to connection. Share your story. Listen to the stories of others. Allow yourself to connect on a deeper level. In doing so, you'll find a strength and a resilience you never knew you had.

## Section 5: Messages of Strength

As we dive into the heart of vulnerability, I want to leave you with some messages of strength. These are affirmations, reminders of the incredible strength and resilience that resides within you. Let these words be a balm for your soul, a beacon of hope in times of doubt.

**You are stronger than you think.** Even on the days when you feel weak, remember that strength is not just about the ability to withstand storms, but also about the courage to be vulnerable.

**Your vulnerability is a testament to your courage.** It takes courage to open up, to let others see your true self. Your willingness to be vulnerable is a testament to your bravery.

**You are not alone.** Even when you feel most vulnerable, remember that you are not alone. There are others who have walked this path, others who understand your struggles.

**Your feelings are valid.** It's okay to feel what you're feeling. Your emotions are a part of you, and they are valid. Don't let anyone tell you otherwise.

**You have the power to heal.** Healing takes time, and it's okay to move at your own pace. Trust in your ability to heal, and know that each step you take is a step towards a stronger you.

**You are worthy of love and respect.** No matter what you've been through, no matter how vulnerable you feel, remember that you are worthy of love and respect.

**You have the right to set boundaries.** It's okay to say no, to protect your space, to take care of your needs. Setting boundaries is a sign of self-respect, and it's a crucial part of being vulnerable.

Remember that vulnerability is not a sign of weakness, but a testament to your strength. As you navigate your journey, hold onto these messages of strength. Let them guide you, comfort you, and remind you of the incredible strength that resides within you.

## Final Thoughts on Being Vulnerable

We've journeyed through the landscape of vulnerability, exploring its many facets and the strength that lies within it. We've acknowledged the courage it takes to open up, to let ourselves be seen in our most authentic state. We've recognized the power that comes from embracing our vulnerability, and the deeper connections it can foster.

Remember, vulnerability is not a sign of weakness, but a testament to your strength. It's a testament to your courage, your authenticity, and your humanity. It's a testament to the depth of your capacity to feel, to love, and to connect with others.

So, as we conclude this chapter, I want to leave you with this message: Embrace your vulnerability. Let it be a source of strength and power. Let it open up new possibilities for connection. And most importantly, let it remind you of your incredible capacity to love and to feel.

You are strong. You are courageous. And you are not alone in your vulnerability. Hold onto these truths as you continue your journey, and let them light your way.

In Her Hour of Need: Messages of Strength & Hope

# CHAPTER FIVE

# EMPOWERMENT: LET'S DIVE IN

You've come a long way on this journey. You've faced the reality of heartbreak, fought silent battles, and begun the healing process. You've learned to acknowledge your feelings and to find hope even in the darkest times. And now, it's time to take the next step on this journey: empowerment.

Empowerment is about recognizing and embracing your inherent strength and power. It's about taking control of your life and your decisions. It's about setting boundaries and cultivating self-belief. But most importantly, it's about realizing that you have the power to shape your own destiny.

In this chapter, we're going to dive into the concept of empowerment. We'll explore what it means, why it's important, and how you can cultivate it in your own life. We'll discuss practical strategies for taking back control, setting boundaries, and building self-belief. And through it all, I'll be sharing messages of empowerment to inspire and uplift you.

Are you ready to embrace your power, to take control, and to become the best version of yourself? If so, let's begin this journey towards empowerment together.

## Section 1: Understanding Empowerment

Empowerment. It's a word we hear a lot, but what does it really mean? At its core, empowerment is about taking control of your life. It's about making decisions that align with your values and desires, rather than being swayed by others' expectations or societal pressures. It's about standing in your truth, even when it's uncomfortable or challenging.

But empowerment is more than just a concept. It's a feeling. It's that surge of strength when you make a decision that's right for you. It's the sense of peace that comes from knowing you're living authentically. It's the confidence that blooms when you realize you're capable of more than you ever thought possible.

In the context of heartbreak, empowerment can be a lifeline. It's the light that guides you out of the darkness, the anchor that keeps you grounded in the middle of the storm. It's the realization that even though you're hurting, you have the power to heal. That even though you've been knocked down, you have the strength to get back up.

But empowerment isn't something that happens overnight. It's a journey, a process. It requires patience, courage, and a whole lot of self-love. But the good news is, you've already started. By picking up this book, by reading these words, you've taken the first step on your path to empowerment.

In the sections that follow, we'll explore the different aspects of empowerment, from recognizing your inherent power to taking back control of your life. We'll talk about setting boundaries, cultivating self-belief, and more. But for now, I want you to hold onto this truth: You are powerful. You are capable. And you are worthy of all the love, respect, and happiness in the world.

## Section 2: The Power Within You

There's a power within you. It's a force that's as unstoppable as the tide, as fierce as a wildfire, as enduring as the mountains. It's a power that's uniquely yours, a testament to your strength, your resilience, your spirit. And it's been there all along, waiting for you to tap into it.

You might be thinking, "Me? Powerful? I don't feel very powerful." And that's okay. It's normal to feel this way, especially when you're dealing with heartbreak. But just because you can't feel your power right now, doesn't mean it's not there.

Think about the times you've overcome challenges in your life. The times you've picked yourself up after a fall, dusted yourself off, and carried on. The times you've stood up for yourself or for others. The times you've made tough decisions, even when you were scared. These are all signs of your inherent power.

Your power is also evident in your capacity to love, to feel, to empathize. It's in your ability to dream, to hope, to envision a better future for yourself. It's in your determination to heal, to grow, to become the best version of yourself.

So, how do you tap into this power? It starts with belief. Believing in yourself, in your worth, in your potential. It involves standing up for yourself, setting boundaries, and making decisions that align with your values and goals. It requires you to take care of yourself, physically, emotionally, and mentally. And it involves cultivating a positive mindset, one that's focused on growth, resilience, and self-love.

In the following sections, we'll explore these aspects of empowerment. But for now, I want you to take a moment to acknowledge your power. Say it out loud, write it down, or simply hold it in your heart: "I am powerful."

Because you are. And this power within you is a key part of your journey towards healing and empowerment.

## Section 3: Taking Back Control

In the aftermath of heartbreak, it's easy to feel like you've lost control. Like your emotions are a wild sea, tossing you about with no regard for your wellbeing. Like your life is a ship adrift, with no captain at the helm.

But here's the truth: You are the captain of your ship. You have the power to take back control of your life and your emotions. And doing so is a crucial step on the path to empowerment.

Taking back control doesn't mean suppressing your emotions or pretending everything is fine when it's not. It means acknowledging your feelings, but not letting them dictate your actions. It means making conscious choices about how you react to your emotions, rather than being ruled by them.

It means setting a course for where you want to go, rather than being swept along by the current. It means making decisions that align with your values and your vision for your life, rather than letting others dictate your path. So, how do you take back control?

First, start by acknowledging where you are. Recognize your feelings, your struggles, your fears. It's okay to not be okay. It's okay to feel lost, to feel hurt, to feel confused. These feelings are a part of your journey, not a sign of weakness.

Next, identify what you can control. You can't control how others act or feel, but you can control your own actions and reactions. You can control how you treat yourself, how you respond to challenges, and how you move forward.

Then, set small, achievable goals for yourself. These could be anything from practicing self-care, to setting boundaries, to pursuing a passion or hobby. The key is to focus on actions that are within your control and that contribute to your wellbeing and happiness.

Finally, practice self-compassion. Be gentle with yourself as you navigate this journey. Remember, taking back control is a process, not a destination. There will be setbacks and challenges, but each step you take, no matter how small, is a victory.

Remember, you are the captain of your ship. You have the power to navigate through the storm, to steer your life in the direction you want to go. And in doing so, you're not just taking back control - you're empowering yourself to create the life you deserve.

## Section 4: Setting Boundaries

Boundaries. It's a word we hear often, but what does it really mean? In essence, boundaries are the limits we set for ourselves and others. They're a way of saying, "This is what I'm comfortable with. This is what I need. This is where I draw the line."

Setting boundaries is a crucial part of empowerment. It's about taking control of your life and your relationships. It's about respecting yourself and demanding respect from others. It's about making your needs and well-being a priority.

But setting boundaries isn't always easy. It can be uncomfortable. It can feel confrontational. It can even feel selfish. But here's the thing: It's not. Setting boundaries is one of the most self-loving things you can do.

So, how do you set boundaries? Here are a few steps to get you started:

**Identify Your Limits:** Think about what you're comfortable with and what you're not. These limits might be emotional, physical, or even time-related.

**Communicate Clearly:** Once you've identified your limits, communicate them clearly. Use assertive communication and be direct about your needs and expectations.
**Stick to Your Boundaries:** This can be the hardest part.

It's easy to back down when faced with resistance. But remember, your boundaries are important and they deserve to be respected.

**Practice Self-Care:** Setting boundaries can be emotionally draining. Make sure to take care of yourself throughout the process. This might mean taking time for relaxation, seeking support from loved ones, or even seeking professional help if needed.

Remember, setting boundaries is a process. It takes time and practice. But with each boundary you set, you're taking a step towards a more empowered, self-loving you.

## Section 5: Cultivating Self-Belief

Believing in yourself is a powerful act of self-love and empowerment. It's about trusting in your abilities, your worth, and your potential. It's about knowing that you are capable, resilient, and deserving of happiness and success. But cultivating self-belief isn't always easy, especially when you're healing from heartbreak.

So, let's talk about how you can nurture this crucial aspect of empowerment.

**1. Acknowledge Your Strengths:** We all have strengths, talents, and abilities that make us unique. Take some time to acknowledge yours. Write them down, say them out loud, celebrate them. These are the qualities that make you who you are, and they're worth celebrating.

**2. Challenge Negative Self-Talk:** We all have a little voice in our heads that can be critical and negative. When you notice this voice, challenge it. Replace negative thoughts with positive affirmations. Instead of saying "I can't," say "I can, and I will."

**3. Set Achievable Goals:** Setting and achieving goals, no matter how small, can boost your self-belief. Start with small, achievable goals, and gradually work your way up. Celebrate each achievement and use it as a reminder of what you're capable of.

**4. Surround Yourself with Positivity:** The people and environments we surround ourselves with can greatly influence our self-belief. Surround yourself with positive, supportive people who lift you up and believe in you.

**5. Practice Self-Compassion:** Be kind to yourself. Treat yourself with the same compassion and understanding you'd offer a friend. Remember, it's okay to make mistakes and have bad days. They don't define your worth or your potential.

Cultivating self-belief is a journey, not a destination. It takes time, patience, and practice. But with each step you take, you're building a stronger, more empowered version of yourself. And that's something to be incredibly proud of.

## Section 6: Messages of Empowerment

As we near the end of this chapter, I want to leave you with some messages of empowerment. These are affirmations for you to carry in your heart, reminders of your strength and your worth. Read them, repeat them, and let them sink into your soul.

**You are stronger than you think.** You've weathered the storm of heartbreak and come out the other side. That takes incredible strength. Never underestimate your resilience.

**You have the power to shape your life.** You are not a passive participant in your own life. You have the power to make choices, to set boundaries, and to steer your life in the direction you want it to go.

**You are worthy of respect and kindness.** Never settle for less than you deserve. You are worthy of respect, kindness, and love, both from others and from yourself.

**Your feelings are valid.** Never let anyone tell you otherwise. It's okay to feel what you're feeling. Your emotions are a part of you, and they deserve to be acknowledged and respected.

**You are not alone.** Even when it feels like it, remember

that you are not alone. There are others who understand what you're going through, and there's always help available if you need it.

**You are enough, just as you are.** You don't have to be anything more or less than you are right now. You are enough, just as you are.

**You have the right to put yourself first.** It's not selfish to take care of yourself. In fact, it's necessary. You have the right to prioritize your own wellbeing.

**You are capable of amazing things.** Never doubt your potential. You are capable of achieving amazing things, and your journey is only just beginning.

Remember these messages. Write them down, say them out loud, keep them close. Because you, dear reader, are empowered. And nothing can take that away from you.

## Final Thoughts on Empowerment

As we wrap up this chapter, I want you to take a moment to reflect on how far you've come. You've navigated the stormy seas of heartbreak, acknowledged your pain, and started on the path to healing. And now, you're beginning to embrace your own power and strength. You're learning to set boundaries, to take control of your life, and to believe in yourself. That's no small feat, and I hope you're as proud of yourself as I am of you.

Empowerment isn't a destination, but a journey. It's a process of continual growth and self-discovery. And while there will be challenges along the way, remember that you have the strength and resilience to overcome them. You have the power to shape your own destiny, to make choices that align with your values and aspirations, and to create a life that reflects who you truly are.

As you continue on your journey, I hope you'll carry these messages of empowerment with you. I hope they'll serve as a reminder of your inherent worth and strength, and of your capacity to overcome adversity and thrive.

Remember, you are not alone. You are strong. You are capable. And you are worthy of all the love, respect, and happiness that life has to offer.

Let's embrace the power within us, and let's continue this journey together. Because in our hour of need, we are not alone. We are empowered, and we are ready to rise.

# CHAPTER SIX

# HOPE: THE LIGHT AT THE END OF THE TUNNEL

If you've made it this far, I want to commend you. You've journeyed through the valleys of heartbreak, navigated the turbulent waters of healing, and faced the silent battles that often rage within us. It's not an easy journey, but it's one that you've undertaken with courage and resilience.

Now, we're going to talk about something that's often overlooked in the midst of pain and heartbreak: hope.

Hope is like a small light at the end of a long, dark tunnel. It's the promise of a new day after a stormy night. It's the belief that things can get better, even when they seem at their worst. And most importantly, it's a vital part of the healing process.

In this chapter, we're going to explore the nature of hope, how to cultivate it, and how it can serve as a guide through your healing journey. We'll discuss the relationship between hope and resilience, and how hope can help you build resilience in the face of adversity.

And through it all, I'll be sharing messages of hope to inspire and uplift you. Because no matter how dark things may seem, there's always a light at the end of the tunnel. There's always hope.

So, let's begin this conversation about hope. Let's explore how it can illuminate your path, inspire change, and guide you towards healing. And let's do it together, with compassion, understanding, and a shared belief in the power of hope.

## Section 1: The Nature of Hope

Hope. It's a small word, but it carries a weight far beyond its four letters. It's a lifeline in the stormy seas of life, a light in the darkest nights, a whisper of possibility in the face of the impossible.

Hope is not just a feeling, but a choice. It's a decision to believe that better days are ahead, even when the present moment is filled with pain. It's a commitment to keep moving forward, even when the path is steep and the journey is hard.

Hope is a spark of light in the darkness. It's the belief that no matter how hard things are right now, there's a light at the end of the tunnel. It's the faith that even in the midst of heartbreak, healing is possible. It's the conviction that even when you're feeling lost, you have the strength within you to find your way.

But hope is not about denying reality or ignoring the pain. It's not about pretending that everything is okay when it's not. Instead, hope is about acknowledging the pain, the heartbreak, the struggle – and choosing to believe that you can overcome it.

Hope is a powerful force. It can inspire us to keep going when we feel like giving up. It can give us the strength to face our fears, to confront our pain, to embrace our healing journey. And most importantly, hope can remind us that we are not alone – that we are part of a community of survivors, of fighters, of women who have walked this path before us and emerged stronger on the other side.

So, if you're going through heartbreak, if you're feeling lost or alone, I invite you to hold onto hope. Because no matter how dark the night, the dawn always comes. And no matter how hard the journey, you have the strength to keep going.

## Section 2: Cultivating Hope

Hope is not a passive state. It's not something that simply happens to us. Rather, hope is something we cultivate. It's a seed we plant in our hearts, water with our actions, and nurture with our thoughts. And just like a seed, hope needs the right conditions to grow

So, how do we create these conditions? How do we cultivate hope when we're feeling lost or overwhelmed?

First, it's important to make space for hope. This might mean setting aside a few minutes each day to focus on the things that bring you joy or comfort. It might mean creating a physical space in your home that serves as a reminder of hope—a corner filled with your favorite books, photos of loved ones, or mementos of happy times.

Second, practice gratitude. Even in the darkest times, there are always things to be grateful for. By focusing on these things—no matter how small—we shift our attention away from our pain and towards the positive aspects of our lives. This shift in focus can help nurture a sense of hope.

Third, use positive affirmations. These are statements that affirm our worth, our strength, and our capacity to heal. They serve as reminders of our resilience and our ability to overcome adversity. Some examples might include: "I am strong," "I am healing," or "I am capable of creating positive change in my life."

Finally, surround yourself with positive influences. This might mean spending time with loved ones who lift you up, reading books that inspire you, or listening to music that makes you feel good. By filling your life with positivity, you create an environment that is conducive to hope.

Remember, cultivating hope is a process. It takes time, patience, and a lot of self-love. But with each step you take, you're nurturing that seed of hope, helping it grow into a source of strength and resilience.

In the next section, we'll explore how hope can serve as a beacon, guiding you through your healing journey. But for now, I encourage you to start cultivating hope in your own life. Because you deserve to feel hopeful, no matter what you're going through.

## Section 3: Hope as a Beacon

Hope is more than just a feeling. It's a beacon, a guiding light that can help you navigate even the darkest times. When you're lost in the storm of heartbreak, hope can be the lighthouse that guides you back to safe shores.

Think of hope as your North Star. Even on the cloudiest nights, when you can't see the path ahead, knowing that it's there can give you the courage to keep going. It's a reminder that no matter how dark things may seem, there's always a light waiting to guide you home.

But hope isn't just about looking to the future. It's also about finding light in the present moment. It's about recognizing the small victories, the tiny moments of joy and peace that can be found even in the midst of pain. It's about learning to see the beauty in the struggle, the strength in your scars.

And most importantly, hope is about believing in yourself. It's about trusting in your ability to heal, to grow, to overcome. It's about knowing that you have the strength to weather the storm, and the resilience to rebuild in its aftermath.

So, as you continue on your healing journey, let hope be your beacon. Let it guide you through the dark times, illuminate your path, and lead you towards a brighter future. And remember, no matter how lost you may feel, there's always a light waiting to guide you home.

## Section 4: Hope and Resilience

Resilience is often described as the ability to bounce back from adversity, to pick ourselves up after a fall and keep going. But resilience is more than just a rebound; it's a transformation. It's about growing through what we go through, about learning from our experiences and emerging stronger on the other side. And at the heart of this transformative process is hope.

Hope is the spark that ignites resilience. It's the belief that things can get better, that we have the ability to overcome our challenges, and that our current circumstances do not define our future. Hope is what keeps us moving forward, even when the road ahead is steep and the journey is hard.

But how do we cultivate this hope-fueled resilience? It starts with acknowledging our feelings and our experiences, just as we've been doing throughout this book. It's about giving ourselves permission to feel our pain, to grieve our losses, and to honor our journey.

From there, we can start to shift our perspective. Instead of viewing our experiences as obstacles, we can see them as opportunities for growth. We can look for the lessons in our pain and the strength in our struggles. We can remind ourselves of our past victories, no matter how small, and use them as fuel for our future resilience.

And finally, we can lean on the power of hope. We can remind ourselves of our dreams and our goals, and use them as a beacon to guide us forward. We can hold onto the belief that better days are ahead, and that we have the strength and the resilience to reach them.

So, as you continue your healing journey, I encourage you to embrace hope and resilience. Remember that you are stronger than you think, and that with hope in your heart, you can overcome anything.

## Section 5: Messages of Hope

As we near the end of this chapter, I want to leave you with some messages of hope. These are reminders for those moments when the tunnel seems too long, the darkness too overwhelming. They are affirmations for you to hold onto, to repeat to yourself, to write down and keep close.

**You are stronger than you think.** You've faced heartbreak and you're still here, still moving forward. That takes incredible strength. Don't ever underestimate your resilience.

**Healing takes time, and that's okay.** There's no set timeline for healing from heartbreak. It's okay to take all the time you need. Remember, healing is not a race, but a journey.

**You are worthy of love.** Heartbreak can make you question your worth, but remember this: You are deserving of love, respect, and kindness, always.

**It's okay to ask for help.** You don't have to face this alone. Reach out to trusted friends, family, or a mental health professional. There's strength in seeking support.

**Hope is always within reach.** Even in the darkest moments, hope is there. It might seem distant at times, but it's always within reach. Keep reaching for it.

**You are not defined by your heartbreak**. You are so much more than the pain you've experienced. You are a person of depth, of passion, of strength and resilience.

**Better days are ahead.** This pain won't last forever. There will be days filled with joy, with love, with peace. Hold onto the hope of those days.

Remember, hope is not about denying the reality of your pain. It's about looking that pain in the eye and saying, "I see you. I acknowledge you. But you do not define me. I hold onto hope, for I know that this too shall pass."

## Final Thoughts on Hope

As we wrap up this chapter, I want you to take a moment to reflect on your journey so far. You've navigated the stormy seas of heartbreak, you've fought silent battles, you've begun the healing process, and you've learned to cultivate self-love and empowerment. And now, you're learning to embrace hope.

Hope is more than just a feeling. It's a beacon that guides us through our darkest times. It's a testament to our resilience, our strength, and our capacity to heal. And most importantly, it's a reminder that no matter how dark the night, the dawn always comes.

So, as you continue your journey, I encourage you to hold onto hope. Let it light your way. Let it inspire you to keep going, even when the path ahead seems uncertain. Because you are stronger than you know, and you have the capacity to overcome anything that comes your way.

Remember, you are not alone in this journey. You are surrounded by a community of women who are walking this path alongside you, each with their own stories of heartbreak, healing, and hope. And together, we are stronger.

So, keep going. Keep healing. Keep hoping. Because in your hour of need, you are not alone. You are seen. You are heard. And you are loved.

# AUTHORS FINAL THOUGHTS

We've journeyed together through the pages of this book, exploring the depths of heartbreak, the healing process, the power of self-love, the strength in vulnerability, the journey to empowerment, and the light of hope. We've had heart-to-heart conversations about the realities of life, the silent battles we fight, and the strength that lies within each of us.

I hope that in reading this book, you've found comfort, validation, and a sense of understanding. I hope you've found messages that resonate with you, words that have touched your heart, and themes that have given you a new perspective.

Remember, you are not alone in your struggles. You are seen. You are understood. And you are stronger than you know. Even in your darkest hour, remember that there is always hope. There is always a way forward. And there is always a strength within you, waiting to be discovered.

As we reach the end of this book, I want to leave you

with a final message of encouragement: Keep going. Keep fighting. Keep believing in yourself. Because you are worth it. You are enough. And you are stronger than any challenge that comes your way.

And remember, this book is always here for you. Whenever you're feeling lost, whenever you're in need of a little strength or hope, feel free to revisit these pages. Let these messages be a source of comfort and encouragement for you, in your hour of need.

# ACKNOWLEDGEMENTS

First and foremost, I want to express my deepest gratitude to the incredible women who have shaped my life and my understanding of the world. To my mother, grandmothers, and aunts, your strength, resilience, and love have been my guiding lights. Your stories and experiences have not only shaped me but have also deeply influenced the words written in this book. I am eternally grateful for your wisdom, your courage, and your unwavering faith in me.

I also want to extend my heartfelt thanks to the countless women who have opened their hearts to me, sharing their stories, their pain, and their triumphs. Your vulnerability and trust have touched me profoundly and have been instrumental in the creation of this book. Each of you, in your unique way, has contributed to the messages of strength and hope that I hope to convey through these pages.

To the women who have reached out to me on social

media, your courage in sharing your most vulnerable moments has been both humbling and inspiring. Your trust in me has been a great honor, and I am deeply grateful for every story, every tear, and every moment of hope that you have shared with me.

Finally, to every woman who picks up this book in search of comfort, strength, and understanding, know that you are not alone. Your journey, your pain, and your healing matter. This book is for you, and I hope that in its pages, you find the solace and the strength you need.

# ABOUT THE AUTHOR

Anthony D. Brice is more than just an author; he is a storyteller, an artist, and a poet who has dedicated his life to exploring the depths of the human experience and sharing his insights with the world. Born and raised in Rock Hill, South Carolina, Anthony's roots have played a significant role in shaping his authentic and influential work.

Anthony's journey as an author began with his debut book, "Poor Me to Soul Rich," a compelling guide to personal growth that has touched the lives of countless readers. His portfolio has since expanded to include a reflective journal titled "My Reflection," a powerful children's book, "I am Powerful, I am Amazing, I am a King," and a guide to self-love, "Loving Alone Until We're Together." Each of these works is a testament to Anthony's commitment to helping others unlock their potential and embrace their unique journeys.

But Anthony's credentials extend beyond his prolific writing career. He is a passionate advocate for education and empowerment, and his work within the literary community has earned him widespread respect. Yet, for Anthony, his work is not about gaining recognition. Instead, it's about making a difference. He seeks to spark conversations, connect with readers, and instigate positive change, one word at a time.

In this book, "In Her Hour of Need: Messages of Strength and Hope," Anthony brings his deep empathy and understanding to the forefront. Drawing from his personal experiences and the countless stories he's heard from women over the years, Anthony offers a beacon of hope for those navigating the tumultuous seas of heartbreak. His aim is to remind every reader that they are not alone, that their feelings are valid, and that healing is always possible.

# RESOURCES

Thank you for joining me on this journey through "In Her Hour of Need: Messages of Strength and Hope." If you found value in this book and wish to explore further, I invite you to check out the following resources:

**Website:** Visit my personal website at **anthonydbrice. com** to learn more about me, my work, and my mission.

**Blog:** For more insights and reflections, check out my blog on Medium at **medium.com/@mranthonybrice.**

**Newsletter:** Stay updated on my work and receive exclusive content by subscribing to The Empowerment Letters at **anthonydbrice.substack.com.**

**Instagram:** Join our online community on **Instagram @ anthonydbrice** for daily inspiration, updates, and a space to connect with others.

**TikTok:** For more engaging content, follow me on TikTok @anthonydbrice.

**Books:** Explore more of my work through my other books. They can be purchased on Amazon.com and wherever books are sold:

*Loving Alone Until We're Together: Discover the 4 Magnets for Maximum Attraction to Manifest True Love*

*Poor Me to Soul Rich: Upgrade Your Mindset to Maximize Your Health, Multiply Your Wealth & Magnify Your Relationships*

*My Reflection: A Journal for Healing, Self-Discovery, and Living on Purpose*

Each of these resources is an extension of my mission to empower, inspire, and uplift. I hope they serve you well on your journey.

Resources